DISCIPLINE
YOUR LIFE TO
SERVE A
RISEN LORD

DISCIPLINE YOUR LIFE TO SERVE A RISEN LORD

Bertha M. Garrett

To order additional copies of this book, contact:
Xlibris Corporation
1-888-795-4274
www.Xlibris.com
Orders@Xlibris.com
20782

CONTENTS

"INTRODUCTION"

Job 36:10a "He openeth also their ear to discipline."
Heb. 12:6, "For whom the Lord loveth he chasteneth,
and scourgeth every son whom he received."
Psalm 94:12a "Blessed is the man whom thou chasten."

Discipline—systematic training or subjection to authority, especially training of the mental, moral, and physical powers by instruction and exercises.

Learning to discipline your life is a process which every Christian should endeavor to do. For discipline requires the best of us. Discipline in our spiritual realm is of the utmost importance in our walk with Christ.

Discipline is a fast, for it requires sacrifices, devotion and a true willingness to serve. Mark 8:34 "Whosoever will come after me, let him deny himself." When we accepted Christ, we began a new walk that must reflect his love in us. Christ redemptive blood has cleansed us from our sin, enabling us to house his Holy spirit. ICor.6:19 "What? Know ye not that your body is the temple of the Holy Ghost which is in you, which ye have of God, and ye are not your own?" Christianity is a daily walk with Jesus. The indwelling of the Holy Spirit opens us to discipline. Without our ears being open to the discipline that our life requires to serve a risen Lord then we are unable to be disciplined properly as a true follower of Christ. A disciple (person) and discipline (training) is two words that have much in common. To be a disciple or follower of Christ we must be trained therefore we are discipline in our walk. Discipline in our daily walk is a necessity. It is the formula for our discipleship.

If our body is the temple then we must take care of the earthen vessel that He has placed His Holy spirit within. The Holy Spirit will not dwell in an unclean house. The Holy Spirit is the instrument of our chastening. Hebrews 12:8-11 As the Holy Spirit chastens us, it opens our ears to self discipline. It gives us that innate desire for a closer walk with God, a more prayerful and spiritual walk with God. It inspires our heart to discipline self.

As a child is chastened by a parent so will God chasten those whom he loves. The proper chastisement of a child has been given us by God. When we chastise, we mold, in molding, we train. Proverb 19:18 "Chasten thy son while there is hope, and let not thy soul spare for his crying." When we administer the rod of chastising, we impose discipline upon the spirit, molding them with godly character, weeding out unfavorable characteristics. As they grow, their ears are open to self-discipline. In chastising we have done as the scripture says: "Train up a child in the way he should go and when he is old, he will not depart from it". How often do we hear a person say? When I was a child, I got the worst whipping of my life because I talked back to mamma or daddy?" We were not allowed to disrespect anyone that was older than we. Our parents demanded respect in their attitudes and walk. And because of that chastising and fear of the consequences our ears were open to the fact that it was far wiser to obey than to disobey. Through this wisdom came the understanding that we as individuals, must discipline ourselves to follow the right and be obedient to our parents. They instilled in us a moral and spiritual discipline that would make us better human beings.

If we truly desire a closer walk with Christ then we must impose self-discipline. Christ did discipline self. Discipline of self can only come through self-sacrifice, denial, devotion, and work. As the Holy Spirit chastens us then we become more obedient to His Will in our lives. Christ at the age of twelve remained at the temple talking with the men in the temple. His parents had started on their journey back home before they had realized that Jesus was not with them. They returned to the temple and found him. His parents not understanding, scolded him. Jesus spoke: "How is it that ye sought me? Wist ye not that I must be about my Father's business?" Luke 3:49 Perceiving that his parents did not understand what he was speaking of: Jesus being discipline in obedience toward his earthly parents subjected his will to their earthly authority as his earthly parents and went with them. This left no opportunity for it ever to be said that he was disobedient in any way. He knowing that there was no place on this earth for him not to be in His Father's presence but he had disrobed His Holy State and became mortal man to live a Godly life without question and without faults so he could redeem the fallen man.

We must seek goals and guidelines in our daily walk. Professional athletes, entertainers, actors and other professional artists have learned to discipline themselves. The football, tennis, hockey, baseball, boxer, and golfer have well-disciplined themselves, mentally, emotionally and physically to endure the rigorous training and torture their bodies must go through to accomplish their goal of physical fitness. The professional entertainers have well-disciplined themselves to master and cultivate their given talents. Actors discipline themselves with studies so that they may take on the characteristics of the person they are to portray. The sculptor must discipline himself to work tediously and skillfully as he molds and chisel his work into shape. A painter has a discipline eye to see beauty that others normally do not see. A writer must learn to discipline their thoughts. All things did meticulously are done with precision and discipline.

A child left undiscipline will disgrace, humiliate, disobey, and find themselves in much trouble in life. A fruit tree left unpruned will stop bearing fruit or the fruit will not be fit for usage and the branches will grow wild. Soil left uncultivated will not produce a crop and weeds will grow. A house left uncleaned will look shabby and uncared for. Land uncultivated, fruit trees unpruned, and houses that are not kept will show others that the person in charge of the upkeep or rather the owner does not truly care or does not take the time to care for the property. When we fail to discipline our children we present to society the attitude of uncaring parents. Failure to chasten our children closes their ears to discipline.

In this book I have been inspired to take daily acts of living and tasks of life and apply them in our discipleship with Christ. Because we serve a living God, one that is not made, but the creator of all living things; we are to live life in a discipline yet a joyous manner; setting us apart from the world. Our service to him should not be somber, nor depressing, neither dead nor inactive. We serve a Risen Lord, meaning his force or power within us surpasses all understanding or comprehension. Life, death, and resurrection are all in his hands.

Christ left His supreme authority and came to a lower position. After his resurrection or rising from the dead he arose to a higher position. Although He alone had the power over death, the sacrifices of animals were accepted as a symbol of the blood that must be offered for man to be free eternally. Christ, the only one worthy, chose to be the sacrificial lamb.

A child at birth comes forth crying or in movement, as the doctors declare it a live birth. Life that which moves and breathes. Anything that rises is doubled in bulk or rank, or in force. A person accepting Christ as their Savior has accepted the afflictions of the cross, the spiritual death of sin and the rising power of the resurrection (a new life). They have a life with greater force, one of a higher rank, one that is double in bulk. His spirit dwelling in us is our leavening because it is a living force that is alive and active.

When we make yeast bread, we have to be careful not to let the yeast shy therefore not allowing the dough to rise or let it get to hot thereby killing the action of the yeast. Yet properly administered and used the dough will rise. After the rising we must knead it with great force to give it the texture that we desire. However with little kneading or no kneading the dough will rise yet the texture of the bread will be different. The kneading makes the dough mixture smooth and shinny. Then after shaping, it rises again and is now fit for baking.

Accepting Christ as our Savior gives us the active leavening we need to rise to eternal life.

This leavening allows us to rise to effectiveness in our christian walk because the Holy Spirit will knead and beat out the gummy and excess bubbles of our life to give us the texture we need to be of service to our God. As this process takes place our ears are open and we no longer have a desire to be of the world. So we must discipline ourselves by the attention we give our spiritual life.

Topics such as the Bonding of Love, the first necessity of being a true Christian, Taking care to Dress spiritually, Cleaning Our House of worldly and unnecessary things are given to show that through our daily walk with Christ: by the chastisement of the Holy Spirit we must Discipline Our Life to serve A Risen Lord. Christ was disciplined in his earthly walk. When rebuked by his parents, he subjected himself to their authority as his parents. When tempted of Satan in the wilderness he was disciplined not to argue with Satan and even in his weaken position physically he was discipline with the word of God. When told at the wedding by his mother that there was no more wine; although he made her aware that his time had not come; Jesus did not refuse to do what his mother requested of him. He stated: John 2:4 "Woman, what have I to do with thee? Mine hour is not yet come." Yet he humbly obeyed and with the discipline of a son and savior he turned water into wine. Before Pilate, although all power was in his hand he was obedient to His purpose and discipline in his actions.

When tempted of satan we must discipline ourselves to be Careful Not to Offend, To Remove the Scalp to Heal the Wound. We must discipline our spiritual self so that we will not be assassins of others character, or reputation. We must be prayerful and work in our vineyard of life, by tilling the soil of our heart.

Christ manifested through our daily walk will inspire others to want to know about him. As we build bridges and follow Jesus we will be able to tell others that when Jesus is on board of our ships in life and when the storms are tossing us about and we cry Master Careth Thou Not That We Perish, He will rise and say Peace be still to our soul.

"BONDING OF LOVE"

Col. 3:14 "And above all things put on love,
which is the bond of perfectness."

Human beings are the product of two unique individuals created by God. Through this union of love so ordained by God, man creates and multiplies his species. No other method has been formulated by which man can be created. We do not understand or comprehend the formation of ourselves through the womb of a woman. Man must plant the seed. The woman is of man and man is born of a woman;[1] a fusion which no one truly understands. We know the act that takes place but what goes into the formation and development of that child in the womb man's intellect has not discovered. The woman though created from man by God is the vessel that God uses to bring mankind into the world. The father nor the child can know each other as long as the baby is in the womb. The mother and father are aware of the existence of the baby in the womb. The mother more so than the father because not only does her body takes on a physical, emotional and mental change but also some chemical changes. With modern techniques of the ultra sound the baby can be seen by the father but he cannot make connection with the child so no bonding takes place with the father until after birth.

It is necessary for this baby after maturing in the womb to come forth through the tunnels of birth to be born. At maturity in the womb it can no longer stay in the mother's womb, so therefore it pushes through the birth canal or rather the mothers body works in unison and pushes the baby forth. The mother expels the baby from her body. This is the birth in the natural sense.

Man through a woman comes into the natural state. However only through Christ can they come into the spiritual state. Jesus is the only way we can have a spiritual birth. Again man cannot understand this birth. Man's only connection with God after the fall and before the atonement of our sin through Christ were through superficial means. Only those anointed of God, could really communicate with him, or come into his presence. God labored with man, suffered for man, and through Jesus obedience through death, he conceived us. In his crucifixion he labored for us, through his death and burial he suffered for us and paid the penalty for our sins, and through his resurrection he gave us life. He birthed us into the spiritual state and claimed us as His own. Ephs. 2:13-16.'But now in Christ Jesus, ye who sometimes were far off made nigh by the blood of Christ. For he is our peace who hath made both one, and hath broken down the middle wall of partition between us; Having abolished in his flesh the enmity, even the law of commandments contained in ordinances; for to make himself of twain one new man, so making peace. And that he might reconcile both unto God in one body by the cross, having slain the enmity thereby."

In the natural state we have no choice as to whether we are born or not. But this second birth we have a choice, he will not force this birth upon us. We must come voluntarily, although he has already made it possible for all men to come into this new birth.

I Cor. 11:8 & 12 "For the man is not of the woman;
but the woman for the man.
For as the woman is of the man,
even so is the man alos by the woman.

John 3:3 & 16 "Verily, verily I say unto thee,
Except a man be born again,
he cannot see the kingdom of God.
For God so loved the world that he gave

his only begotten Son,
that whosoever believeth in him
should not perish, but have everlasting life."

At birth man is presented his child, before he touches it, it is cleansed and wrapped, then he is allowed to hold it and bond with it. Although the mother is very much aware of the changes in her body, and the bonding is there, only after birth when the child is placed in her arms is there a true bonding of love. The mother often holds and touches the baby before it is cleansed but she cuddles it more once it is cleaned. The more she holds it, the more she loves it, the more protective she becomes the more nurture she gives. The more the father sees it and bonds with the child the more protective he is. As the child grows the love bond between parent and child grows. The bonding of love is forever there but the physical ties can be broken through death.

Although God our Father created us, and knows all about us we do not get to know or bond with him until we are born of Christ. John 14:6b Jesus said: "No man cometh unto the Father, but by me." When we are washed and cleansed from our sins through the blood of Jesus Christ then we are placed in the loving arms of God where even death cannot sever us from his love. Romans 8:35, 38, 39 "Who shall separate us from the love of Christ? 'For I am persuaded, that neither death, nor life, nor angels, nor principalities, nor powers, nor things present, nor things to come. Nor height, nor depth, nor creatures, shall be able to separate us from the love of God, which is in Christ Jesus." The more we grow the more we love him and the closer we desire to walk with him. The more we grow the more we rejoice in pleasing him and giving him the glory in our lives. We no longer waver as a new born, but have complete faith that God is able to supply all our needs. Though in the worldly state he provides for us, he even more so provides and cares for us as we are his divine children. Ephss. 1:11 "In whom we have obtained an inheritance, being predestinated according to the purpose of him who worketh all things after the counsel of his own will. That we should be to the praise of his glory, who first trusted in Christ." Verse 12.

When we are bonded in love through the blood of Jesus Christ, we are no longer of this world but rather bonded eternally in the love of Jesus.

"CLEANING HOUSE"

2 Chronicles 29: 15b-16a
"By the words of the Lord to cleanse the house of the
Lord, And the priests went into the inner part of
the house of the Lord to cleanse it."

Isaiah 1:16
"Wash you, make you clean; put away the evil of your
doings from mine eyes."

In the early spring we give our houses a thorough cleaning. We clean out closets, basements, refrigerators, freezers, wash winter coverings, turn mattresses, beat out rugs, shampoo carpet, and walls, thereby giving our house a complete cleaning. We clean with products that will leave our house smelling fresh and clean. We use detergents and softeners to make our wash smell fresh. For extra freshness often we hang many things outside so that they may get the freshness of the spring air. At least once a week the house is given a thorough cleaning. Yet sometimes no matter how we clean we still have odors. Often it is something that we should have thrown away but decided to keep for sentimental reasons. Items that are usually stored in our basement where moist has caused an odor to form. Things in the attic do not cause odors like those stored in the foundation of the house.

In the old testament the priests were given the order to cleanse the house of the Lord removing all uncleanness. In the New Testament we see Christ before his death went into the temple cleaning out that which was not right. After his death and resurrection we see that our body is His Temple. I Cor. 6:19 "Your body is the temple of the Holy Ghost which is in you. "I will dwell in them and walk in them and I will be their God and they shall be my people. 6:20 "For ye are bought with a price therefore glorify God in your body." We are admonished to glorify God in our body, and in our spirit, which are God's. The Temple in which he dwells is not built by hands so we must realize that this price is too high for us to pay. The earthly temple in which he dwells is our body and he created it so we must work to keep it clean before the Lord. In the old testament the priests took the uncleanliness that he found in the house of God and took it to the brook of Kidron; so that it would be washed away. Jesus blood is the brook that washes away our uncleanness of sin, to allow the Holy Spirit to dwell within.

We should completely clean our houses, by washing out our closets of fear and doubt, our basement of envy and jealousy, our refrigerators of ill feelings, our freezers of grudges and revenge, wash our coverings of unforgiveness and mistrust. Turn our mattresses of hate, beat out our rugs of gossip and backbiting, wash our walls of fault finding, shampoo our carpets of nick picking to give our house a complete overall cleaning. We must use products that will leave our house smelling fresh and clean.

Often when we pass a house the outside looks very clean. The lawn maybe well manicured and the best of care may have been given to the outer portion of the house. Yet there is something that detracts from it. The house may look dark and foreboding or beautiful but not happy. Flowers surrounding it, but they are all artificial. A house can have all the aspects of prosperity but no laughter or joy. It can be the largest mansion on the block and have all the trimmings that say wealth is within but not conducive to happiness. Sometimes this is the way it is with those who profess to be christians. They attend church every Sunday and go to prayer service but each time you see them they seem to have no joy. People are afraid to approach them because their greetings are always short and snappy or sometimes they ignore you completely. Some may have high positions or highly educated, large community influence, great material wealth, in much favor with the authority of the church, and great family lineage in the church, that the common everyday member is beneath them. Because some members do not have furs and dress as well as they do or have the family clout that they do these members are looked down upon or frowned upon. These church goers are well manicured outside but the insides are dark and foreboding and their hearts are surrounded by artificial flowers. Their church walk have the aspect of prosperity but no laughter or joy. Their church activities are many with trimmings but not conducive to happiness. Unless the house is cleaned within and The Holy Spirit abides therein we cannot truly show forth the joy of Jesus Christ.

Matthew 23:26 "Cleanse first that which is within that the outside may be clean also.

That simply dressed Christian with no education or very little former language and the one that shout at the mention of Jesus is known by the joy that they show and the happiness that exudes from them. Because their talk betrays them, for they have been cleansed within. We look through our windows of deception with self righteousness seeing all the ugliness that surrounds us but not realizing that often the smear is one that is found within ourselves. When we wash the windows of our deceit then we can get a clearer view of others.

We must throw out the old clothes of apathy, slothfulness, inattentiveness, disrespect, so we can get rid of the hidden odors. "Cleanse thou me from secret faults." Psalm 19:12b The hidden faults that are within our hearts and minds such as unforgiveness, jealousy, envy and mistrust hinders us from having true joy in Christ. We must learn to discipline our lives so that we can be and will be prayerful in our daily life. Getting rid of the hidden faults will enable us to show forth the inner working of the Holy Spirit, the true joy of living for Christ and not the exterior joys of the world or the superficial happiness of material possessions. Things that are hidden are covered up with deceitfulness which can cause us much unhappiness. For those who cannot and will not forgive will never truly be happy, nor will those who hold grudges ever have peace in their lives.

We can only be truly cleansed by the blood of Jesus Christ. Once that cleansing takes place and we learn to study His Word and allow the Holy Spirit to work freely in our lives then we can be properly disciplined in our walk with Christ.

"TAKING CARE TO DRESS"

Matthew 15:8-9a
"This people draweth nigh unto me with their mouth,
and honoureth me with their lips,
but their heart is far from me.
But in vain they worship me."

Each day when we prepare for our jobs, we take care to dress, clean and fashionably. We take baths, comb and style our hair, brush our teeth, and for some apply make up. Taking care that no offensive odors are about our persons. We dress to please ourselves and others. We dress to make a statement for this is the carnal man within. But how do we dress the spiritual man? Do we take care to make a strong presentation of our spiritual selves? Or do we dress our spiritual self as we do when we just want to lounge around home or simply don't care? Do we start our day off by bathing thoroughly in prayer asking God to purge our heart of all uncleanliness and unkind thoughts or deeds? Do we attire ourselves fashionably with God's word or haphazardly not caring how we look? Do we apply our make up by seeking his divine guidance, wisdom and understanding? Showing forth Jesus in us, in our inner and outward appearances. Did we comb out the lent, dandruff, and smooth out the kinks in our lives and ask God to forgive those who wrongfully use us, not allowing us to judge another?

Taking care to dress our spiritual self will not allow us to feel envy toward another. Taking care to style our heart with humbleness before God, putting on a protective shield. Did we brush our teeth by asking forgiveness of our sins? Did we rinse our mouth thoroughly of untruths? Taking care to dress ourselves for church, for being in the presence of the Lord. Spraying on the perfume of love, human kindness, compassion and patience so when we meet or greet others our fragrance will be pleasant and pleasing. And as we embrace our sisters and brothers in Christ a little of our fragrance will touch them making it a joy to be in fellowship with one another. Unless we clothe ourselves with the appropriate attire for worshiping then we worship in vain. Going into the house of prayer or worship full of anger and hatred toward our fellowman hinders us from true worship. If our mind and spirit do not have on the correct clothing and we search out our fellowman seeking who to talk about or nick picking as to the outer clothing that person may have on then we are as dead bodies in the house of worship.

To dress properly takes discipline. When we greet the public, have we disciplined ourselves to make the right impression? Whether it is a smile that is sincere or a smile that hides hurts or disappointment. When dealing with the public, we must not allow the pain to show. When we are representing Christ, we must not allow our cross to show in our presentation, we must show forth His presence in us. In the house of worship we must be clothe with his Holy Spirit so that we can feel the joy of worshiping him. John 4: 23-24 "But the Hour cometh, and now is, when the true worshipers shall worship the Father in spirit and in truth, for the Father seeketh such to worship him." God is a Spirit: and they that worship him must worship him in spirit and in truth. We cannot have on the attire of the carnal man to worship our God. We cannot bring that which is of the world into our house of worship for the invisible edifice of our heart is where our worship service begins. Our first forms of dressing must be that of regeneration or rather being born again. We must believe that Jesus is the Son of God. John 3:16 "For God so loved the world that He gave His only begotten Son, that whosoever believeth in Him should not perish, but have everlasting life. Once we accept Christ as our personal savior we must seek a more personal relationship with him by studying his word. As we study his word and learn of Him We become shielded with the whole armour of God. Ephesians 6:13-19" Wherefore take you the whole armour of God that ye may be able to withstand in the evil day, and having done all stand. The armor of God is an entire attire your loins become girded with truth, putting on a breastplate of righteousness, our feet will be shod with the preparation of the gospel of peace, taking on the shield of faith, being able to quench all the fiery darts of the wicked. Putting on the helmet of salvation and the sword of the spirit, which is the word of God. This attire will keep us in prayer and supplication not just for ourselves but for others in the work of God and his utterance will be given to us for our well being and for other saints.

"LOOKING BACK AND BECOMING A PILLAR OF SALT"

Genesis 19:26
"But his wife looked back from behind him,
and she became a pillar of salt."

How many times in the course of a day are we asked to forgive someone? Peter asked this question of Jesus: "how oft am I to forgive my brother? till seven times?" Jesus saith unto him "I say not unto thee, until seven times: but until seventy times seven." Matthew 18:21-22. The one who is asked forgiveness of has a greater task than the one who is forgiven. The forgiver must learn how to forgive and pray that God will heal the wounds. Often this is not easy.

Many times the wounds are open sores and are constantly exposed to objects that prevent the healing. However when we consider that as we walk this journey our life must reflect the one who died for us all we can look at the fact that many wrongs are open wounds to him. These wounds are abominations to him yet at calvary he said Father forgive them for they know not what they do . . . Still the offender of him must ask for forgiveness and repent of that sin. When we ask Christ to forgive us, He does not look back at our former sin. As He told the woman that was to be stoned; "neither do I condemn thee, go and sin no more."

When you forgive someone who has wronged you, they immediately feel better. However, in time their conscience will condemn them. When we ask Christ to forgive us, we have a cleansing feeling of relief that floods over us yet sometimes we condemn ourselves with regret for that which we have done. So many times the one that has wronged you has so much pride that they cannot or will not seek or ask forgiveness. It seems as if they are still being blessed even though they have wronged you. If you can look beyond that exterior appearance and say I forgive even if they don't ask and ask God to forgive them then that wound will not go untreated.

When God opens the storehouse of your blessings and brings you out of a bad situation don't look back on what you think could have been or might have been. Just forgive yourself and those that have wronged you and pray for them. Pray for the healing of your land. Lots' wife was being asked to leave the place where she had raised her children; a place she had no doubt grown to love, a place that held precious memories for her some good and some bad so she looked back.

Looking back is often a sign of regret for that which you are leaving and that can take you and keep you there. When Lot's wife looked back, she became a pillar of salt. Looking back in our lives or on the wrong that have been inflicted by someone can cause our heart to become a pillar of salt. Because we start wanting revenge, start wondering why are they allowed to prosper seemingly at our expense. We start harboring the false conception that they owe us something that they deserve to suffer as we think they have caused us. True we may suffer because of some wrongs that have been done to us but we cannot undo the wrong but through Christ we can use it for our good. Lots' wife never knew what happened as a result of her looking back but it left her husband and daughters alone to dwell in the mountain of Zoar, in a cave. Her daughters perceiving that they would not have a man nor would their father have a seed left him, slept with their father after making him drunk with wine. Looking back, often causes a person, to lay blame causing them to become bitter and resentful. This attitude will be nourished into our children and those that are around us because our heart has become a pillar of salt and not filled with love.

We must learn discipline in our actions toward others as we strive to be more Christ like. When we are wronged by someone be it a christian brother or sister or one in the world we can be certain that God will avenge.

Galatians 6:7 "Be not deceived; God is not mocked: for whatsoever a man soweth, that shall he also reap." We must pray for those who misuse us or do us wrong and in so doing we reap blessings upon ourselves and coals of fire upon our enemies.

Pro.25:22 "For thou shalt heap coals of fire upon his head, and the Lord shall reward thee." When called out of our cities of sin and given a chance of eternal life we must be obedient and not look back.

Looking back on wrongful acts done by others to us can only cause our hearts to harden toward that person thereby not showing forth the love of God in us.

"TAKE UP THY CROSS AND FOLLOW ME"

Matthew 16:24
"Then said Jesus unto his disciples,
if any man will come after me, let him deny himself
and take up his cross and follow me."

We are admonished to take up our cross and follow Jesus. Before dying on the cross, Jesus, bore his cross aided by Simon, a Cyrenian, and on him they laid the cross, that he might bear it after Jesus. Luke 23:26b. The cross, that consists of intersecting lines, forms a structure that becomes a burden to the one that carries it. And bearing his cross He went forth to a place called the place of the skull. John 19:17. We as christians, form our cross when we decide to follow Jesus. In following him the intersecting lines of carnal and spiritual form our cross. We must deny ourselves, refusing the untruths of the world and accepting Christ as the only true and righteous way.

Self will be placed upon that cross many times but as we follow Jesus the wings of his mercy and love will quickly blow self off. The cross of self-denial that of greed and pride will not have room as we tread to calvary. Our crosses sometimes are formed by others when we are trying to live right before God, and sometimes we will help others bear the cross. So we must keep our eyes on the one whom we are following in order to bear our cross effectively. If we take our eyes off the leader we may walk blindly into obstacles or get a beam in our eyes. However as we follow him, although we meet with stumbling blocks they cannot hinder us. Christ has already cleared the way we need only to trust in him. He will give us the strength to climb our mountains; the courage to push back the stumbling blocks, the ability to walk around or go over the obstacles in our path. The longer we walk with him the sooner we realize that the power is in his name and that we must learn to give him the praise.

As we journey on this path sometimes, our cross seems to be so heavy that we wonder how can we carry it. We question the fact if we are truly following in Jesus footsteps. But if we keep on following him these footsteps merge into one and our cross becomes lighter as we grow stronger. Our cross allows us to grow in faith as we began to realize that not only does he walk in front of us, leading us, guiding us but that he is beside us supporting us, carrying us, and encouraging us, and behind us giving us that extra push to keep on going. We then look beyond and see a cross with one looking to heaven and our eyes immediately look upward. When we look up, our thoughts are taken from self and instead we look at the one on the cross. We no longer feel the burden of the cross but the joy and wonder he gives as we follow him. Every step that Jesus took on earth was leading him to calvary. When we chose to follow him every step we take from that day leads to calvary. At calvary Jesus was placed on the cross and was lifted up. At our calvary in life we will be placed upon the cross and be lifted up, not beside him, not before him, and not behind him, but in him and then we shall see glory. Only through him can we be lifted up and if he is lifted up he'll draw all men unto him.

When we accept Christ as our savior, we automatically take up a cross. How we bear this cross requires discipline in our spiritual walk with him. Denying self as Jesus admonishes the ones who desire to follow him is the first form of discipline a Christian must adhere to.

"BE YE NOT NARROW"

Isaiah 54:2
"Enlarge the place of thy tent,
and let them stretch forth
the curtains of thine habitations:
spare not, lengthen thy cords,
and strengthen thy stakes."

We often sing the song just like a tree planted by the waters, I shall not be moved. Psalm 1:3. The tree that is planted by the water has many branches and leaves; oftentimes spreading for out over the water. The roots are deeply embedded and the tree grows upright stretching proudly casting a shadow over all that passes by. Even through the changes of the seasons it still looks healthy.

True we as christians should be as that tree, but instead we become narrow. Afraid to outreach to others, afraid to cast our shadows, to allow others to get close, afraid to nourish upon the flowing river of God's love and allow it to pour out to others. We become so engrossed with ourselves, our groups, our talents, our churches, and other involvements, that we forget we are members of a larger and greater church, that is the invisible church of Christ.

We look around and see how those of the world spread themselves to touch the lives of others, how they influence others, whether good or bad. But we as christians sometimes have the attitude of jealousy in our midst, making us narrow, unable to spread and flourish. We hesitate to greet a stranger in our midst. We are afraid to welcome a new member with open arms. Afraid that they may come into our domain and take that which we feel we have accomplished. Not realizing that any and all gifts that we have are given to us by God.

Christians should be able to draw others unto Christ. As the tree shades others along its' path, we as christians should be able to shade others with love. Each tree that is planted by the water forms an umbrella that enfolds each other, protecting all things that come beneath or into their branches.

Christ love forms an umbrella that covers and protects all his children and that love within us should extend outward to touch others. Everywhere Jesus went there was a crowd. The path we travel is a narrow one but there are many people we will meet along that path. Although we take the narrow path, we ourselves, our spiritual selves, should not be narrow. Psalm 1:3 "And he shall be like a tree planted by the rivers of water, that bringeth forth his fruit in his season; his leaf also shall not wither; and whatsoever he doeth shall prosper." For in our season, in our time of life in Christ, our time of service to him should not wither. Our deeds should not wither for as we grow so should our leaves and fruits. So that when our harvest of life comes our storehouse will be filled. If we as christians stretch forth our arms of love and seek to draw others unto Christ then that which we do will prosper. We should not be narrow minded toward others. We should not be narrow in our heart, or be narrow with our forgiveness, nor with our love, smiles, or thanksgiving. Christ gives liberally of his love, forgiveness, mercy, and grace; drawing people into the love of Jesus Christ.

In order for us not to be narrow minded or narrow in our heart, we must be true disciples of love, the love that cannot be encompassed with narrow mindedness or limited by a begrudging heart. We ourselves are limited in this area of love, but through Christ, in His word, through discipline we can grow in the agape love. Studying his word teaches us the discipline we need when the world says be unforgiving. We will forgive; when the world judge, we will judge not, when our brother or sister in Christ falls we will be the first to lend a helping hand and pray for them. Knowing that where some are weak others are strong and with true discipline we will pray for the edification of our sisters and brothers in Christ.

"THE ASSASSIN"

I Peter 4:15a
"But let none of you suffer as a murder."

Many times we suffer persecution just because we are christians. But what about the persecutor? Paul was an assassin. He persecuted christians. Steven was stoned to death because he lifted up Jesus. Jesus was murdered because he was the Son of God. He was killed by those that were called or chosen by God to be his people. He was killed by those of the world who thought themselves to be righteous. Paul not only persecuted christians physically but imprisoned them also.

There are many ways by which to be an assassin. Through jealousy, hatred, the lack of temperance, and envy. When we are jealous of someone, we try to destroy their character and influence. Through hatred, we seek to destroy physically. By lack of Temperance we assassinate ourselves; we over indulge in gossip, ready to tell the mistakes and downfalls of others. We criticize our fellow Christians when we permit satan access to our thoughts then we quench the Holy Spirit and will not allow his spirit of love to flourish within us.

The bible tells us that "He who hideth a matter seeketh love. But he who seeketh to destroy another will tell the matter whether it is true or not, to kill the spirit of another or destroy his or her influence." Prov. 17:9 Let none of you suffer as a murderer. We kill more than just physically. Oftentimes as Christians we kill more with our tongue. We must pray that we do not become assassin's of another spiritual influence. We must lift our brothers and sisters in Christ up in prayer daily not giving way to jealousy or envy.

Joseph's brothers were jealous of him and they sought to kill him but instead sold him to the Ishmeelites. Yet this action caused Israel, Joseph's father much sorrow because he was deceived into believing that the son whom he loved was dead. We as Christians can sometimes cause the harm to another by the favoritism we show toward another even though others maybe trying as hard. We give the praise to the one we favor and over look the efforts of others, thereby quenching the spirit of one that could truly be a blessing to us. David's lack of temperance would cause the death of a man and the death of an infant son. We must learn to discipline ourselves in our spiritual life so as to give godly praise to the efforts of others not showing division amongst ourselves as Christians. We must learn and practice temperance in our daily walk, so as not to cause harm to another.

Those who are spiritual leaders must lift up the word of God in action and deed as well as with words. "For as a man thinketh in his heart, so is he". Pro23:7 We must ask ourselves how many times do we in our carelessness with the use of words or with our thoughtlessness do we quench the spirit of another that is truly trying to serve God. If our deed offend someone and cause them to be discouraged in their walk or deeds then we are guilty of wounding that person spiritually.

In our christian walk we must not let positions, nor gifts, talents or wanton desires, make us envious or mistrustful of another's walk with Christ. There are those who may be more spiritually intoned with prayer, there are those that are more diligent in their walk, those that have stronger faith, those with gift of words, eloquent and charismatic in speech, those with voices of angels, or those that have no specific gift to the eyes of man and just devoted church members, whatever the gift, it is of God. For whom much is given much is required. The greater the gift the greater hurt of bearing that gift. That person with the greater gift have more labor in birthing those gifts than those that have one. As a woman in childbirth labors to birth a child into the world so must those with spiritual gifts.

We must rid ourselves of that spirit of jealousy, being critical or judgmental. Because in so doing we assassinate the character of those that are our sisters and brothers in Christ. Think what a disgrace it would be to kill our biological siblings, or how destructive it would be to the family. So would it be with our spiritual family. It takes discipline to not allow the evil tongue of gossip, backbiting or criticism to be a part of our spiritual selves. Because we as Christians often judge others by what we suppose to be right and therefore if one does not act in the framework we think we criticize. Some to the point of thinking that if one act different from the way we act then they are wrong. But we can not look into the heart or know what is right in the eyes of God.

We must learn how not to find fault in the service others seek to give.

"LIFT UP JESUS"

John 12:32
"And if I be lifted up from the earth,
will draw all men unto me."

All Christians must lift up Jesus in their daily walk. Only when he is lifted above us can we give him glory and praise. If we lay him down in our lives then no one is able to see him and we trample upon him. If we lift him beside us then self may obstruct the view and he is not seen in us. If we lift him front then we may become pushy and others only get a glimpse of him in us. If we place him on our backs then we give someone the impression that we are caring him. However if he is lifted up from the earth, not beside us, not behind us, or beneath, or in front, or on our backs then nothing obstructs the view of the cross in our lives. The eye immediately goes to that which is above, that which towers over us shinning his light upon us. When one is drawn to look up, onlookers become curious and they began to look up. Curiosity about what enables beams of light to radiate from one hanging on the cross draws others to see the light.

When Christ is lifted up in our trials and tribulations, when he is lifted up in our troubles, pain, and heartaches, then we don't look at the situations but rather look up to the cross. Making onlookers wonder how do we press on despite the misfortune in our lives they become curious as to the message we portray in our walk. Then they want to know more about the man we profess to serve.

Christ, glory can only be shown through us when we lift him up in our walk him up in our walk. Self can never be seen in our efforts of discipleship. When we have truly been with Jesus and lifted him up in our lives our speech and walk will show it. Peter's speech betrayed him when question if he was with Jesus or if he knew Jesus. Although he denied it, the man stated: "Surely thou art one of them; for thy speech bewrayeth thee." Matt. 26:29 Being hung on the cross beside Jesus looking at him made one thief believe saying: "Lord, remember me when thou comest to thy kingdom." Luke 23:42 Lifting up Jesus in our lives bring forth action, because when he is lifted up the earth can not rest. When others see what he has done in our life as we lift him up, how he can move mountains for his children then they like the centurion and others at calvary will believe. Math. "Now when the centurion, and they that were with him, watching Jesus, saw the earthquake, and those things that were done, they feared greatly, saying, Truly this was the Son of God."

It was in his being lifted up that brought them to their knees in belief. That is what we must do as Christians lift up Jesus at all times. Soul winning can not be done through our worship services but rather through our daily walk and daily services as a christian. It was on the cross at calvary that the centurion and others believed. But still in Christ daily walk he drew men unto him with his words, with his deed, with his walk, with the radiance that shown from him. Our daily walk in Christ is to lift up Jesus. To lift him up daily is to show forth his glory through us.

"REMOVING THE SCAB TO HEAL THE WOUND"

JOB 34:6b
"My wound is incurable without"

Often we as Christians are hurt and wounded in our spirits. Especially when we are trying to do the will of God. The more we serve him the more we are open to the snares and darts that are aimed at us. Many times the hurt comes from those we love and trust most. These are wounds that cannot be healed without.

If we cut ourselves with a knife or some other sharp object we immediately cleanse the wound. However no matter how much we clean the wound if the blood is not good or there is some other problem surrounding that area the wound will not heal properly. Our bodies have a natural antibody that causes our wounds to heal themselves. If these antibodies are not sufficient then we may have a problem as far as the wound healing process. Then sometimes the wound forms a hard scab but the surrounding area is still sore or inflamed especially the area beneath the scab. If we brush up against something the wound can cause us much pain. So we must remove the scab in order to heal the wound. When the scab is removed the wound is immediately exposed to air and it begins to heal.

When we are hurt or wounded spiritually, sometimes we do not take care to treat the wound properly by cleansing it of germs that have infected the area. This wound can only be cleaned by prayer and his word. Though we may verbally say we forgive; the scab of unforgetfulness forms. The wound is still tender and subject to infections. However if we remove the scab of

41

unforgetfulness, we allow the air of love to circulate and cleanse the tenderness of mistrust and the infection of apprehension. Although this wound can only be healed from within we ourselves do not have the proper antibodies to sufficiently heal the infected area. Unless we are prayerful and have been feasting upon his word, the wound will form a hard scab and tenderness will be within. His word is the antibody that will work from within through the Holy Spirit to heal our wounds. A wounded spirit can't be healed by soothing words of an apology. But if cleansed thoroughly with his word, and washed with prayer, then soothed with love, the wound can be healed. We must remove the scab to heal the wound of discouragement and an unwillingness to serve.

The life of a christian is often filled with wounds caused by fellow christians. And many times we may hurt our fellow christians unintentionally. Therefore, we must learn to discipline our language and actions. In our spiritual family we wound with our tongue more than with actions.

In order to heal the wounds caused by others or prevent from wounding another we must discipline our ears to the word of God. Discipline our heart with love and forgiveness. Discipline our minds with good thoughts toward others and always remember that Christ forgave us. When we have disciplined ourselves with these thoughts we will not wonder how much are we to forgive. The hard crust of unforgetfulness will not allow our wounds to heal. So we must pray that as we forgive God will make the memory only a thought. The act of forgiveness allows us to grow spiritually therefore closer to him. The soft scab of envy and jealousy can form into hard crust of resentment causing our wounds not to heal properly. If you leave these wounds unattended and believe they will heal on their own they will eventually grow into a hard scab. This hard scab is not easily removed because often times we are not aware of the fact that it is there. We lack growth in our spiritual walk, we see others full of joy, we see those that seem to have a great peace despite their circumstances and we wonder why or what can we do to gain this relationship in Christ. This soft scab of envy and jealousy has grown so hard that it has become a part of our every day life so that it does not seem to hurt and we blame others for our unhappiness and our lack of joy and peace. Envy makes us begrudge another and jealousy makes us want that which another has or wish that person did not have it. These attritubes slowly but surely destroys a man. It is a difficult situation for man because he himself cannot heal these wounds or remove these scabs. All that we need is in Jesus and to be properly healed of any wounds we must use the prescription that is given to us in the word of God. When we seek to apply this medication to our wounds, whether it is the soothing salve of love or the healing power of forgiveness and love, or the comforting and refreshing act of grace and mercy then we can expect the healing of our wounds.

"MASTER, CARETH THOU NOT THAT WE PERISH"

MARK 4:35-40
"And he was in the hinder part of the ship asleep on a pillow; and they awake him, and say unto him, Master, careth thou not that we perish."

When Jesus told his disciples to go across to the other side he did not say there would be smooth sailing; but rather that they were to go to the other side. In going across to the other side a storm came up. The wind and the waves beat against the ship the disciples became afraid because they were not able to guide the ship safely through the turmoil of the sea. As the wind and the waves began to rock the boat they became fearful that they might perish.

Jesus lay calm and serenely asleep. The winds and the waves did not awaken him. The cry of his disciples (master careth thou not that we perish) was what awaken him. Jesus had told them they were going across to the other side. If only they had remembered that promise, then they could have rested comfortably without fear but with the certainty that although the way was rough they would make it to the other side. Jesus sensing their lack of faith did rebuke the wind and the waves and said: "Peace be still." verse 9. It was their peace that had been disturbed, the peace and tranquility of the sea disturbed. Although there was anxiety amongst the disciples and the wind and waves beat against the ship Jesus merely said peace be still. In other words I restore peace to your mind to the sea and to the wind. The peace of the universe that was surrounding the disciples and

Jesus was being troubled. Jesus lay sound asleep on the ship knowing that he would safely reach his destination. The disciples knowing that Jesus had directed them to go across had become fearful because of their lack of faith. Yet they knew that Jesus could help but they did not understand that with Jesus on board no harm could or would come to them. When Jesus spoke peace be still fear no longer tugged at their heart, the disquieting of the mind was no longer aggravated by fear that they would perish. When Jesus grants His peace calmness and security will surrounds us.

The storms of life do not touch Jesus, nor do they trouble his spirit for the storms must be. However in the storm, if His child cries out for help and our peace is disturbed then he hears us. Our cry touches Him when we ask if he cares whether we perish beneath the turmoil then he grants peace. But only when we allow him to work for us in faith. The sea of turmoil and the winds of life will beat against our ship, as we cry out master, careth thou not that we perish. When he says peace be still the turmoil to our life will cease because the wind of trouble will obey his will. The waves of tribulation will obey His voice. The storms of fear, doubt, anxiety, distress, and worry will subside. Jesus will restore our peace and we can go safely to the other side.

How does peace come to us? When life's ship is tossing us about and we cry master, careth thou not! It comes when we have fervently and earnestly prayed and abided in his word. When his word has become our substance of survival and we learn to lean on him for this daily bread, our faith will grow and we can safely trust him to take us to the other side. But our ears must be intoned with the Holy Spirit relying on its guidance. We must be open to the word by carefully studying so that when we cry out, that which we have fed upon and that which have nourished our soul will sustain us.

"PLANTING TREES AROUND THE ALTAR"

DUET. 16:21
"Thou shalt not plant thee a grove of any trees
near the altar
Of the Lord thy God."

Trees, one of God's most magnificent creations are deeply rooted in the earth, but grows straight up to the heavens. Trees have many beneficial purposes that are knowledgeable to man. They purify the air we breathe, beautify our surroundings and give shade and comfort to our surroundings. We cut trees in the forest, or woods, to build homes, make paper, and many other products and purposes. There are herb and fruit bearing trees. Trees that are essential to the well being of our environment as well as having many medicinal purposes. Trees supply homes and shelter for many animals and birds.

As beautiful as they are, trees can also be quite harmful. The roots of trees can be most damaging to a dwelling. They can cause much damage to our sewage system and drainage. In cases of storms they can if blown down and uprooted crush or destroy our dwelling. The roots although deeply embedded in the earth, sprouts and entwines with other tree roots, so much so that the roots to one tree may never be removed.

Branches on trees grow out so that they form umbrellas over their surroundings. The seedlings from one tree quickly sprout wherever it is blown. God made the trees and the trees always honor its' maker by being obedient to the Masters' Will. Wherever God place it, it will grow.

Then why not, if the tree has so many good qualities plant groves around the altar? As we know when we are in the woods or forest, we cannot see clearly, nor can the sun shine upon us sufficiently. We are hidden from the eye of man and many things can and do dwell in trees, such as: snakes, birds, beasts, and other wild creatures. Nothing can be hidden from God's view but the heathens had worshiped all the hosts of heaven in their groves; with enchantments, dances, and other unholy forms of worship. They made their sacrifices in the midst of the groves. God did not desire his people to take on any of the heathen ways or forms of worship. He had instructed Moses, how he wanted his altar of sacrifice to be built and who would be allowed to offer the sacrifices.

We no longer have the temple as described in the old testament because the holiest of sacrifices have been made for the atonement of our sins. Now the temple dwells within us. "His Holy Spirit gives us the utterance we need to communicate with the Savior. We must not plant groves around the altar of our heart. When we allow jealousy, bitterness, envy, hatred, hostility, pride, gossip, and evil conduct to seep in we are planting groves around our altar. Christ purchased the altar of our heart with a price unequal to any that man can make." I Cor. 6:20 "For ye are bought with a price therefore glorify God in your body and in your spirit which are God's The roots of jealousy, lies, hatred, anger, and pride can quickly grow into our pipes of faith, prayer, and love. Sprouting seeds of untruthfulness, disrespect, dishonesty, gossip, assassination and separation. It can divide the body of Christ in the visible sense. Sometimes we must dig deep to find the cause of our lack of spiritual growth or the cause of our pipelines of prayer, and faith being clogged up; or the dwelling of our faith and joy to be obstructed. Oftentimes the trees damage our property only in times of severe storms but the roots are a constant hazard to our dwelling. The outer damage can easily be replaced but the damage done by the roots causes much labor and effort. Therefore we as Christians, must discipline ourselves to not allow groves to be planted around our altar. The sprouts or seedlings from other trees can so easily blow over and take root around the altar of our heart.

Listening to gossip about our spiritual leaders, or sisters and brothers in Christ allow thoughts to enter our mind. Thoughts that are seedlings from another tree. If we are not careful and prayerful then we can readily become soil for that seed to grow. We must discipline our thoughts with his word, our heart with his love, our spirit with his spirit, so that no seedlings can sprout up within our spirit. The roots of jealousy can kill because they will choke out the effort of praise of others. When we plant trees around the altar of our heart, we may never see the sunlight. Christians, must keep the word of God in their heart and the shield of His Spirit will protect us.

"BUILDING BRIDGES"

I Cor. 3:10
"According to the grace of God which is given unto me,
as a wise master builder, I have laid the foundation,
and another buildeth thereon.
But let every man take heed how he
buildeth there upon."

Christ was a perfect constructor, he built a bridge that we can safely cross over the rivers, highways, mountains, and valleys of life. A bridge that has a firm foundation and without any flaws. V.11 "For other foundations can no man lay than that is laid, which is Jesus Christ." He laid a foundation that cannot be washed away by the floods of life, one that will not give way to the weight upon it, nor sink, or be destroyed by bombs; or by any other means satan or man may seek to destroy. The bridge is so well structured that it is a safe passage for whomsoever travels across.

As we walk on this road of life, we too will build bridges. For we are laborers together with God: Ye are God's husbandry, (or tillage) ye are God's building. Verse 9. Christ laid the foundation but we also build upon the bridge. We are admonished to take care as to how we build upon the foundation laid by Christ Jesus. Every man's work shall declare it, because it shall be revealed by fire: and the fire shall try every man's work of what sort it is." Verse 13.

Many times when a young child is asked what does she or he wants to be, or who would it like to be like! They always say someone that has influenced their lives, someone that is visible to the eye, not someone that they cannot see.

When we teach our children about Christ, do we lead an example that they can see and feel His love and mercy? Or do we give an example that Christians are always oppressed and down trodden? Do we build bridges of victory, of faith, of good stewardship? Works that can be tried by fire and abide. V.14. "If any man's work abides which he hath built thereupon, he will receive a reward." Men such as Abraham, Joseph, Moses, David, Jacob, Job, Peter, and John built bridges tried by fire and withstood. Abraham built a bridge of faith, Joseph built one of endurance, Moses built one of leadership and as one who walked with God, David built one of courage, Jacob built one that changed his name therefore a nation was born unto him, Job built one of patience and faith, Peter's faith was a rock, John was a witness, and Paul, a great preacher. But they were all built upon a firm foundation and that foundation is Christ Jesus.

Those who desire to cross over on the bridge we build must see Christ as the foundation so they too can build. If we project self on our bridges then we have not built upon the foundation of those gone on before neither can we build upon the foundation of Christ. Self must be denied and all worldly principles because Christ is the only one that those who follow us must be able to see.

"TILLING OF THE SOIL"

Pro. 12: 11 & 12b.
"He that tilleth his land shall be satisfied with bread;
And the root of the righteous yieldeth fruit."

Farmers in the early spring check their soil; look over their land to see the damage that harvesting and winter freezing have done. They remove the debris of winter, the dead limbs, twigs and branches.

The farmer knows that he must take proper care of the land that he possesses. A farmer is usually a humble man, who knows that farming is a tedious work of love. He knows the tasks that he must perform to maintain the land. He tills the soil to put it in order for production of crops. The crops by which he receives his food and supplies his livelihood. This soil has to be cultivated so as not to go to waste. He knows that soil left unattended would soon become wasteland.

After removing the debris he will plow the land, and then harrow it, leveling the plowed ground and breaking up the clods. The soil is fertilized, making it fit to be sown. Everything that has caused the soil to be unfit for planting has been taken care of and the farmer has taken care to give it the proper nutrients that will cause the land to be fertile. Proper care of the soil ensures the farmer of a productive crop. His labor of preparing the soil will not be in vain.

We are the soil in which God plants His Holy Spirit. God labors in love toward us, he cultivates us to remove the debris in our lives, so that we can grow in his love, mercy, and grace, making us as Christians humble in prayer always seeking his face. As we till our lives with fasting and prayer, to remove the garbage of the carnal self, the broken glass of bitterness that become cutting edges, the dead twigs and branches of jealousy, resentment, unforgiveness, and deceitfulness we are preparing our soil for proper seeding. The Holy spirit is the turning mechanism that cultivates us. Plowing and breaking up the clods of disrespect, gossip, selfishness, and peace breaking. As we allow the Holy spirit to harrow us, we can hoe with faith and be fertilized with his word. Since our life is bought with a price our soil is only lent to us, so we must take care. I Thess. 4:4 "That every one of you should know how to possess his vessel in sanctification and honor." Proper tilling of our soil will give honor to the planter.

We as the farmer must know how to till the soil with love though the task maybe tedious. We must study his word so that our soil may be fertile. As we are used by the Holy Spirit, our desires will be toward God, causing us to turn from our wicked ways allowing him to heal the land of our heart. 2 Chron 7:14 "If my people, which are called by my name, will humble themselves and pray, and seek my face, and turn from their wicked ways: then will I hear from heaven, and will forgive their sins and will heal the land."

When we have tilled the soil of our heart then God will heal our land making it fit for produc-tivity. Proper care of our soil will make us walk honestly before them that are without that we will lack nothing. I Thess. 4:12 Tilling our soil will ensure us of a fruitful yield. A fruitful yield not only in the life to come but while we walk on this earth. It will give us peace on our journey and a closer walk with God. Our harvest of love will be bountiful. Our storehouse of humblenes meekness, kindness, and love will allow us to be better Christians and stewards of that which God has entrusted us with. With proper care our harvest will be plentiful.

"PULL OFF THY SHOES"

Ex. 3:3
"And He said, draw not nigh hither;
put off thy shoes from off
For the place whereon thou standest is Holy Ground."

Shoes are used as a covering and as protection for our feet. They protect us, warm us and help us walk better.

Often we come into the house of God laden with thoughts that we should n have. These thoughts cover us, shield us, and help satan in preventing us from enjoying and receiving the blessings that are in store for us when we come into the house of God. So as Christians we should put off our shoes from off our feet before entering the house of God.

Before we come to church we should pray that we leave our earthly cares and worries, and dislike of someone, our disappointment, our judgmental attitudes, our observation of others, our mistrust, our thoughts of things past, present and future, if they are not intoned with the spirit. We must put off the shoes of doubt, worry, fear, and anxiety, impatience and disrespect.

When growing up we were often told by our parents or grandparents to pull off our shoes before entering the house. In certain countries the custom is still to remove your shoes before entering the dwelling. Out of respect one would comply. Our parents did not want us to track the dirt in from the outside so the floors could stay clean longer.

We cannot come before God with coverings that are unclean

with the soil that we trample in day by day, that are sweaty and odorous. The sanctuary of our heart should be clean. The vial of our mind should be free, so that when we enter the sanctuary of God; we can come boldly in our worship of him. We can greet our sisters and brothers in Christ with joy and jubilation, so the spirit of God can flow freely in our midst. Unless our shoes are removed, we are not fit to come upon His Holy Ground. The coverings of envy, jealousy, strife, malice, criticism, and disrespect must be left outside the door of our heart.

Oftentimes on Sunday mornings in our rush to get to church we are anxious, over tired and frustrated with the efforts of trying to get to worship service on time. The first place many of us go is to the wash room to make sure our hair, dresses, stockings, suits and ties are straight. Then we mingle with our acquaintances or friends speaking of things that happened during the week or last Sunday. Before entering the sanctuary we have on the heavy shoes of gossip, observations and other things we need not have on. We must discipline ourselves to remember to pull off our shoes of gossip, worry, mistrust, and observation before entering the inner sanctuary. The inner sanctuary of our hearts must be open and receptive to the blessings and workings of the Holy Spirit. When we are truly open to the teachings of the word of God, we have nourishments that will supply us for our daily living.

"THE ROD CHOSEN OF GOD WILL BLOSSOM"

Num.17:5a &8b.
"And it shall come to pass, that the man's rod,
whom I shall choose,
shall blossom: and, behold the rod of Aaron
for the house of Levi was budded,
and brought forth buds, and bloomed blossoms,
and yielded almonds."

There is a choice given to man, that of salvation or that of eternal damnation. In choosing salvation we choose to serve and follow Christ. In following Christ we are given certain tasks and those tasks are anointed by him.

Although Israel was a chosen people of God, and they suffered much affliction in the land of Egypt; God did not call every Israelite to deliver themselves from Pharaoh's oppression. He had a lamb in the bush and that lamb was not raised amongst the children of Israel. He was raised in the household of Pharaoh as his grandson. When Moses sought to defend his people himself, the thing was made known and he had to leave his homeland and flea from the sight of Pharaoh. However over the process of time forty years, God saw fit to go to Moses in Midian where he had fled and called him service. He was the rod chosen of God to free his people from Pharaoh's oppression.

Moses communed directly with God; he was chosen as a leader for God's people. But Aaron was anointed to perform the priestly duties of the temple and to offer sacrifices upon the altar. Although he performed the priestly duties he was not in the presence of the Lord as was Moses. Moses was the one that God would allow to come unto him.

David said to be a man after God's own heart was anointed as king over Israel. He was not a prophet but rather a warrior for the Lord. When he desired to know an answer from God, he sent unto a prophet of God, for God's word. He respected the anointing that God had placed upon each individual in his life. Even the anointing of Saul, though Saul sought to slay him. Before he was anointed king, David, was a skillful musician. His skill was blessed to be used of God, to glorify and give him praise. He became a great song writer. He organized the first choir for the service of praising God. David was not a priest, but he was anointed of God. David was a man of great courage and God blessed him mightily.

A tree may have many branches but all may not bud or bare fruit. Some trees may bud at the appropriate time but do not bare fruit. Before it blossoms, the buds fall away. Man often sees someone they may like and desire to raise them up in a position. This person may or may not have the skill but is trained and yet cannot rise above that level of opportunity. The rod may grow and bud but it does not blossom or bare fruit. Saul was anointed as king over Israel because they desired to have a king. Although chosen of God he was anointed as a request for a king, by God's people. Saul's rod grew and budded it also blossom, but fell away before it could bare fruit. Saul did not bare fruit; he is remembered as the first king over God's people and the one who tried to kill David. However David when chosen as king did blossom and bore fruit. He is remembered as the one after God's own heart, as a man of courage, a great warrior, the greatest song writer yet to be known, as one who knew deeply of repentance, heartaches, trials and tribulations. But more importantly often when we speak of Jesus, we say that he is the seed of David. How precious was the fruit of David.

Moses the one chosen of God to lead his people out of Egypt. Moses's rod was chosen and it budded, blossom and bore fruit. The one that had a oneness with God. One who walked humbly before God, and was obedient to the will of God except for one occasion. It was Moses that God would inspire to write the first five books of the Bible. Moses was given the Ten Commandments in the mount. He is called the lawgiver.

The rod chosen by God though in the midst of others and despite all that man may do to hinder, will still bud and blossom. The rods that each man held up were sticks with no life for they had been taken from the source of life. Life was restored to the rod and it brought forth buds and bloomed blossoms, and yielded almonds. God can choose one that is dead and bring it to life and raise it up to bear fruit. When God chooses to bring forth a rod, it will honor the Son and glorify the Father.

As we grow in Christ, we must keep our ears open to know what it is that God desires of us and not that which man desires us to do. Nothing that we do that it is not of God will bare fruit.

With our ears open our attitudes toward our brothers and sisters will blossom with love and forgiveness. We will become more humble in our walk. Our spirit will be that of a meek and lowly one and not desirous of the praise and recognition of man. When we have done our best to please God, it does not matter if man is pleased or if he gives you praise because God will let you know that he is pleased. Our Christian walk will blossom and others will see that the Holy Spirit dwells in us and that God is working through us and it is not of ourselves. It is not enough that we blossom but rather that we should also bare fruit. As we grow and blossom our fruits of love, forgiveness, humbleness, peace, human kindness, encouragement, devotion, and meekness will flourish. These fruits will reap us a great harvest, inspiring others to accept Christ as their Savior. Discipline in our Christian walk allows us to bare the fruit of righteousness and faithfulness.

"PURSUIT OF EXCELLENCE"

HEB.12:1b
"Let us lay aside every weight, and the sin which doth so
easily beset us, and let us run
with patience the race that is before us."

Phil. 3:8-9
"And I count all things but loss for the excellency of the
knowledge of Christ Jesus
My Lord, and be found in him, not having mine own
righteousness."

Let us run with patience the race that is set before us. But as we run this race let us work, for the perfection of our task. We as Christians have taken on a race for eternity; one that will be laden with many obstacles. However we are admonished to run this race with patience and not with haste. We must strive to be the best at our calling as we are the ones whom the light of Jesus shines through. If we take on a task and pursue it in haste, often we will make mistakes and sometimes overlook something that is vital to the success of our endeavor. Saul pursued David in haste not conceiving that David also was an anointed child of God, thereby Saul made many mistakes and was twice delivered into David's hands. Moses became impatient with his people enslavement and killed a man as a result. However his people were not freed and suffered forty more years after this incident. At the water of Mer'ibah Moses disobeyed God and struck the rock therefore he nor Aaron was allowed to go over into the promised land. Numbers 20:7-12.

Not having mine own righteousness. How easy it is for us to

allow the successes we acquire become more important to us than the souls that are saved. If our edifice that we worship in is large and paid for we often are grateful for the fact that we are able to raise the money to make it possible. But Christ ministering on this earth was seldom done in the temple but rather along the highways and by ways of life. His disciples learned from him by the works that they saw him do and from his daily teaching and from being in his presence. They were not eager to venture out on their own. Realizing that they were not yet equipped to do the works that they saw Christ do.

It is not that we are not to do work in the visible church but when we have a charge in our life the Holy Spirit will use its chastising rod to prepare the inner man for the work that he must do for Jesus. On our part it will take patience, but yet we are to study and show ourselves approved. 2 Tim. 2:15. "Study to show thyself approved unto God, a workman that needeth not to be ashamed, rightly dividing the word of truth."

And I count all things but loss for the excellency of the knowledge of my profession. Students, teachers, doctors, lawyers, scientist, writers, poets, entertainers, actors, and athletes, all have one thing in common; they desire to be the best in their area of studies and professions. To reach the accolades of their professions they must pursue the cause with diligence. Rarely does anyone no matter how gifted, achieve any amount of success in their profession without honestly pursuing it. When one is seeking to master a profession, all things that may hinder are counted as a loss. Nothing or no one will or can prevent them from striving to achieve their goal in life.

Teachers may desire to return to school to obtain a master or doctorate in a given field of study. The B.A. gives them the right to teach because they have learned well their given subject. A master say's I've striven to be a master of knowledge of my profession, opening up new areas of opportunity. A doctorate tells you that I specialize in what I'm doing. I've acquired a degree of knowledge in my profession that allows me to be an authority on the subject. Some in given professions are bestowed honorary doctorates in life, not that they've gone to a university, but rather that they've been schooled well in the learning process of their profession by experiences. They know what they do better than anyone else. Often those that study at universities can learn from those who have striven long and hard to be the best at what they do. Entertainers often do not have degrees from universities for the knowledge they've learned from experiences but they do know their business better than anyone else.

Professional athletes are people who strive to master the art of playing the game a certain way. Dancers and actors strive to master their profession. Writers and poets have their own style of writing and expressing themselves. Newsmen have their own way of delivering the news that makes them appealing to the public. Doctors, lawyers, scientists, engineers, all study to master their profession. We as Christians must always pursue to be excellent in our walk with Christ. Yet there are times when we must not strive but be patient. 2 Timothy 2:24 "And the servant of the Lord must not strive, but be gentle unto all men, apt to teach, patient." When obstacles are put before us by other Christians we are not to become angry but rather be patient and pray for them. In our prayers God will help us to overcome the obstacles. Although we do not give up the pursuit of excellence for in this trial, we are still in that pursuit. Working to be our best in following Christ we will and must encounter obstacles, trials, and tribulations. But our battle must be done in prayer not with resentment or force, not with malice or hatred. Not with the thought of vengeance or victory but rather with the love and patience of Christ Jesus.

Christ pursued the excellence of our salvation and nothing hindered him. He had no hatred, or bitterness toward us because of our fall neither did he pursue our salvation with resentment, but rather with love. Nothing man said or did, prevented him from achieving his ultimate goal. Not temptations, nor false accusers, or unbelievers, not denial, betrayal, persecution, or death for he pursued the excellency of our salvation in obedience and love. When betrayed and he knew death was at hand he did not flee or allow anyone else to be harmed. John 8: 7,8, & 10b-11. "Whom seek ye? I have told you that I am he: if therefore ye seek me, let these go their way. Peter having a sword drew it, and smote the high priests' servants' ear off. Then said Jesus unto Peter, "Put up thy sword into the sheath: the cup which my Father hath given me, shall I not drink." Even at the hour of capture his thoughts were not of self but for those around him and for what he must do to redeem man from Satan's hold. At the last hour before death he was still thinking of those who wronged him and ask that God would forgive them. Luke23:34 "Then said Jesus, Father, forgive them; for they know not what they do."

As we journey in our pursuit of excellence sometimes, it is necessary for us to go to calvary. We must learn the ultimate of forgiveness and love. We must not see our hurts, or the wrong done to us but rather that when Christ work is hindered it is done to Christ and we are only the vessels by which he is performing the task. When at the cross Jesus love will not allow us to put self first nor will it allows us to be in his presence with envy, hatred, or unforgiveness. The more we pursue excellence the more love we will have toward our fellow man.

Mark 8:36 "for what shall it profit a man if he shall gain the world, and lose his own soul?" If we do not follow Jesus we are lost, and if we follow Jesus we must deny self. So all things are counted loss except the things found in him. Because only the works that we do in his name are counted as gain.

"TO CAUSE OTHERS NO HARM"

I Chronicles 21:17
"And David said unto God, Is it not I that commanded
the people to be numbered?
Even I it is that have sinned and done evil indeed;
but as for these sheep, what have they done?
Let thine hand, I pray thee, O Lord, my God,
be on me, and on my father's house but not on thy people,
that they should be plagued."

Many times when we say or do certain things we never stop to think of the harm we may cause others. The saying "It's my thing I do what I want to do"or "this is a free country and I can say what I want to say," is a carelessness on our behalf that can cause love one to suffer. Often times the innocent suffer for the wrong doings of others. Because of one man's disobedience we all have fallen and one man's obedience and lack of sin we all have a right to eternal life. Romans 5:19 "For as by one man's disobedience many were made sinners, so by the obedience of one shall many be made righteous."

All that we do affects others directly or indirectly. When a person steals, he takes away something that another has worked hard for or something they may treasure. An unfaithful husband causes much pain and suffering to his family. He neglects them and often they must go without to satisfy his pleasures. Children abandoned by father or mother must rely on others, state, or streets for their food, shelter, and clothing. These children often feel unwanted.

The Spirit of God does not allow us to carelessly hurt others. However many times because the carnal man still exist and we are only mortal and subject to be used by satan our actions and deeds still can hurt others if we are not careful. Therefore we must learn to discipline ourselves as not to cause others harm.

David was tempted of Satan to number the people. When he committed adultery and killed Uriah, Bathsheba's husband, the evil was brought upon his household. He lost an innocent child and one of his sons rose up against him. However with the evil of numbering the people, he had caused harm to many of God's people. David had a chose of three things that could happen, and he must choose one. Three years famine, or three months to be destroyed before his foes, while the sword of his enemies over took him, or three days the sword of the Lord, even the pestilence, in land. Nos 21:12 "David said unto Gad, the seer I am in a great strait: let me fall now into the hand of the Lord; for very great are his mercies: but let me not fall into the hand of man." Even in this David allowed God to make the chose because he believed in Gods' mercy. But when David saw the sword of the angel stretched out over Jerusalem he fell on his face.

Had David listen to the advice of Joab and not numbered the people then the seventy thousand men of the Israelites would not have fallen. However when he saw the evil he had done he asked that he fall in the hands of God and not into the hands of man. David repented and cried for God to spare Jerusalem.

If our eyes were open to see the harm we cause others by our tattling, backbiting, deception, and gossip then we would ask God to stay his hand. If we could see the destruction caused by jealousy, hatred, and envy; then we would pray that God forgives us and that we would not cause harm to our fellow Christians. We would pray that God would stay our tongues and evil actions toward our fellowman, reaping destruction upon the spirit of new converts, and offending those who are working in the vineyard with us. We cause harm to their spirit and their efforts of service. Sometimes we slay their works by our evil actions and evil tongue.

If we pray constantly and study his word; His word will convict us when we are wrong and do others wrong. And we like David will cry out and repent and desire that we do not cause others harm. We Christians have destroyed the influence of many that are in Christ because of our jealousy, our desire of favoritism and our lack of the word of God.

"THE OFFERING OF STRANGE FIRE BEFORE THE LORD"

Leviticus 10: 1-2
And Nadab and Abihu, the sons of Aaron,
took either of them his censor,
and put fire therein,
and put incense thereon and offered strange
fire before the Lord,
which he commanded them not.
And there went out fire from the Lord,
and devoured them, and they died before the Lord."

Fire in the old testament was used in sacrifices, for purifying in offering, as a protective shield over the children of Israel. Aaron and his sons were admonished not to offer up strange fire. They themselves must be holy and clean in their lives in order to offer up the daily sacrifices.

Fire was used on the altar continuously. The fire that was offered up in the temple must be offered reverently to the Lord. It was to have a sweet savor. Only the priest was allowed to offer this fire upon the altar. They were given strict methods by which to do the sacrifices. It was given by God through Moses his servant.

In the wilderness on Mount Sinai it was used as a writing instrument for the law of the old testament symbolizing the presence of God. Fire was used to draw Moses to a bush that was not consumed and from this bush Moses heard a voice. The fire on the altar was sacred. It was that by which God received all of his offerings.

When the sons of Aaron offered up fire in their drunken state committing sin rendering them unfit to offer up fire on the altar. Instead of God receiving that foreign fire it returned upon the men who offered it and consumed them. God used this fire as a divine vengeance and purging.

All things offered up to God are to be Holy. We as Christians are not without sin but through Christ we are made Holy. Through His blood we are consecrated upon the altar and the fire of his love and grace burns continuously upon the altar.

Yet there are many who offer up strange fires and they too profess to be Christians. Those that are given the task of caring for the things of God sometimes offer up strange fire. Our bodies are the temple of Christ so we must therefore be careful of the sacrifice we offer upon the altar of the our heart.

We must take care of the surroundings we allow our bodies to be in. As Christians we must search ourselves and pray for guidance. So our gifts of praise will be worthy sacrifices on the altar. Some are busy working in the visible church as pastors, teachers, ushers, deacons, choir members, or the one that greets you at the door. They greet you with God bless you and shout and sing songs of praise, but some are adulterous, fornicators, drunkards and on drugs and many other secret ways of life. Whereby they are deceiving self but not God. They are not putting on the pure beaten oil of olive at the altar. Their fire of praise will not be one of blessings but rather one of consuming. There are many ways to be consumed with fire but none the less there is a consumption. Our influence, our work of faith, our marriages, our homes, our children, our health and our lives can be consumed by offering up strange fire unto the Lord. We must worship God in truth and in spirit. If we are living a deceitful life then we cannot worship in truth or in spirit because His Spirit cannot and will not abide in and unholy place. I Cor 18a-19 "Flea fornication. He that committeth fornication sinneth against his own body. What know ye not that your body is the temple of the Holy Ghost which is in you, which ye have of God, and ye are not your own.'

We must be careful how we teach our children, for they learn from our action. We must seek to discipline and correct them when they become involved in the wrong things or participate in environments not becoming a christian. Eli hesitated to correct his sons when they made a mockery of the sacrificial offering to God. I Samuel 2:12-17 "wherefore the sin of the young men was very great before the Lord; for he abhorred the offering of the Lord". We hurt the body of Christ when we allow our children to become children of the world. Forgetting to teach them to respect or honor the House of God. We fail to discipline or correct our children and allow them to do and say as they please. Elias' house was cursed. I Samuel 2:27-36 verse 29 "Wherefore kick ye at my sacrifices and at mine offering, which I have commanded in my habitation: And Honourest thy sons above me, to make yourselves fat with the chiefest of all the offerings of Israel my people?" The House of God is to be a place of prayer and worship. Today we've brought everything else into His house. Our worship services have become more worldly than sacred. It has become more prone to drawing crowds than nourishing and healing souls.

We'd rather follow the rules dictated to us by man in discipline and training our children than the laws given by God for rearing our children. Comparing where our society is today with our children, as to where it was many years ago when our forefathers believed in biblically training our children we will see an exorbitant difference. Failing to discipline our children causes much shame to our homes, society and churches. Discipline is necessary for the heart, home and well-being of children and self opening the ears of understanding, obedience and respect.

"TO BE PREPARED FOR SERVICE"

John 6:9
*"There is a lad here which hath five barley loaves
and two fishes:
but what are they among so many?"*

A woman is given nine months before she becomes a mother. But the preparation of motherhood starts much earlier. The preparation of learning starts the day of creation. When each child is conceived that mind is developing. The development of the brain that constitutes the mind is formed. As a child grows that body is being prepared for service. A woman's body is prepared for the service receptor of man. Innate instincts are there to know that we are to be of service to each other. All the things are done and made by a divine creator. At the right time our bodies are made ready to be of service for that which God has created it for.

However, it is up to man to make ready to be of service to God. No one says why this young lad had the five barley loaves and two fishes. Whether the mother prepared the meal or the lad himself. Neither does it say how old he is. But the most important factor is that he was prepared to be of service. No one else had thought to bring food for their journey or their stay. As we often in life go out unprepared for the circumstance, we may find ourselves in.

As parents we know that it is always wise to carry a first aid kit incase of an emergency. Yet many times we neglect to or forget to bring along those essential items. And at the time least expected we are not prepared to service our needs.

In reading our bible we see where many men of God went through their wildernesses, trials, tribulations, losses, red seas, fiery furnaces, and lion dens, being prepared for the services of God. It is so very important that when each individual accept Christ as their personal Savior that they prepare themselves to be of service to the Lord. We must learn to discipline our bodies, our mind, soul and spirit to be of service. Sometimes we do things not knowing why but for some strange reason we get a desire or spirit of prayer for someone. In these circumstances we have been prepared to be of service to God. Praying for someone else's need and not being asked or not even knowing what the need of prayer may be.

There are times we have the urge to call or talk to someone we haven't spoken to in years, but at that moment that person may need an uplifting thought or a kindness that God has allowed you to give. These things come by with a close personal relationship with God. So in time of need He may use us. When Jesus passed by a fig tree and desired fruit and the tree was not bearing he cursed the fig tree. The tree was green and full of life but it bore no fruit and could not be of service for the purpose Jesus desired of it.

This young lad had the necessary provisions to be of service to Jesus. It seems as if he willingly gave of that which he had without questioning. Giving it to Jesus blessed a multitude of people with much left over for the lad. The young lad knew that what he had could not feed anyone but himself. Yet though hungry he gave up that which he had and through Christ 5,000 souls were fed beside women and children. Seeing this miracle, more than just the physical hunger of man was fed but the soul of man also. That is why it is so important to study the word of God to strive to have a personal relationship with him so in time of need we can be of service to God. Let us not be like the fig tree, full of life but no fruit to be of service to satisfy Jesus hunger.

Jesus hunger is great today for us as Christians to help others, to tell others of his love, to show others the way, to give our testimony. Some may never come to the visible church or know how to read but we can be a living testimony. All that we do should be preparing us for service.

Abraham's journey in the wilderness before he reached the promise land was preparing him for that one great act of faith in offering his son Issac as a sacrifice. Moses birth, being reared by Pharaoh's daughter, the slaying of the Egyptian, fleeing into the wilderness, all things were necessary to prepare him to be of service to God. David being chased by Saul, being persecuted, living in caves, were training his spirit to be of service to God. Each man had learned discipline. So that they could become worthy servants of God.

"DECEIVING WEEDS"

Matthew 13:30
"Let both grow together until the harvest: and in the time
of harvest I will say to the reapers
gather ye together first the tares and bind them
in bundles to burn them:
But gather the wheat into the barn."

A true gardener is one that can differienate between the weeds and flowers. However sometimes he will allow the weed to remain in the garden until it is safe to remove the weed.

When you are in your garden in the early spring there are many weeds that can be deceiving to the normal eye. Many times these weeds will look much like the flower it is surrounding but a discipline eye can discern the weed from the flower. Yet sometime that weed is allowed to grow because the weed can be so entwined with the flower. In the early spring there are some weeds that have pretty colored flowers if allowed to continue to grow they will choke out the growth of the flower yet they will soon weaken and die away if the flower take full growth. Some weed's roots are very strong and entangled and some are very weak but the weed itself spread faster above ground. Many times you have to pull very hard or dig very deep to uproot a weed. Especially the dandelion weed. The weeds will grow faster and overtake your garden if you do not work swiftly.

There are some weeds that grow in bunches and look like the phlox family while they are young and before they bloom. Blade grass can look like the tender growth of a gladiola, you have to wait a few days before you can distinguish. As much as we try we can not rid the garden of weeds completely. We have to work diligently in our garden giving the plant time to grow in order to survive it's surroundings. As the plant grows the flower or fruit that it will bare will start to form or take shape and it will become stronger than many weeds. However there are weeds that grow faster and much stronger than the fruit they will take over your garden and you must search to find the fruit or vegetables.

The dandelion although this weed have some medicinal purposes will swiftly spread in your yard and overtake your grass. Its' roots are very deep and hard to completely get rid of if not taken care of in time. There is a weed called crab grass that grows slowly but can destroy your grass.

Sometimes Christians allow themselves to get in surroundings that seem harmless. Listen to music that is said to be gospel, enter into conversations that start off with a good point and become involved with people that seem to have good intentions. However the deceiving weeds of their conversation will cause our christian walk to be stifled or stunted in growth or killed if we are not clothe and have not been properly fed with the word of God. When born again Christians are new in Christ we must be careful to teach them properly and to watch the things that we allow to surround them. As parents we are to be careful of the people, music, conversations, and surroundings we allow our children to be in. We as a christian family should tell those that are new in Christ to seek to study the bible and attend Sunday school as well as bible class. But it is even more important to tell them to read their bible daily and pray because deceiving weeds are every where. Being clothe and properly fed with the word the deceiving weeds will be uprooted, die away or choked out. The word of God can gather the deceiving weeds from around our heart and bind them and cast them into the fire to be burned. Only the disciplined eye of the Holy Spirit can pluck out those weeds of deception. The weed of criticism can easily grow around our heart because we can find fault in our christian brother and sister thinking it is okay because we say a little criticism is good for the growth of that person. The weed of doubt can grow swiftly if left unattended in prayer. The weed of jealousy can choke out and kill if allowed one inch of growth. The weed of self-righteousness will kill our spiritual life if we do not remember that we all have sinned. This weed will overtake all of our gardens because we began to look down and find fault in so many of our christian family as did the Sadducees and pharises. If not discipline our christian walk will be greatly hindered.

"THE TOLL ROAD"

Ezra 7:24
*"Also we certify you, that touching any of the priests
and Levites, singers, porters, Nethinims,
or ministers of this house of God,
it shall not be lawful to impose toll, tribute,
or custom upon them."*

Toll—a fixed compensation for some privileges granted or service rendered.

Life itself demands a price. If we chose salvation eternity with Christ is our reward. If we chose to remain in our sin and reject Christ eternal damnation is our reward. But there is a fixed compensation Whatever choice we make there is a price one is paid for us and the other we pay for. The price of damnation is high for we have allowed our souls to be held in eternal bondage to satan which is death eternal.

In life God has so ordained that we have choices. If we accept the plan of salvation, then we have no toll to pay but we have a price to pay as we travel along this road. A toll road is paid to get to a certain destination that you can not get to on a regular road. Salvation is a set destination that we cannot arrive at unless a toll has been paid. That toll is paid by Jesus and the price for us to get on this road is His life. Once we get on this road changes take place. Their is a fixed compensation one that is not according to the size of car, or your monetary standards, nor is it fixed according to your influences in life, or your family lineage but by the blood of Jesus Christ.

After or rather upon entering this toll road you will find there are exits and by passes on this road. The exit of self must be ultimate, the exit of jealousy, doubt, fear and worry must be sincerely prayed to exit from. We must by pass the temptation of sin, gossip, idol worshiping and backbiting. As long as you are on this toll road even if you exit, you can be sure that all you have to do is repent and seek forgiveness of your sins and turn around and access to the toll road again will be given. Some time you get on one of the by passes and you get lost every other exit lead you further and further away from your destination and the only way you can get to the designed point is to stop and ask direction and turn around. There are no back ways once entering the toll road you must pay to get off. On this christian walk if you desire to get off this toll road you will pay a price that you don't have the funds to repay.

If you choose to travel the well traveled road to reach your destination you can exit and never get back on for there is another route. Traveling South you can take 65 or 75, one maybe longer or the bluegrass which is a toll road. Along these roads are many beautiful sceneries. Many tempting places to stop, many areas of pleasures and leisure time. Remember you don't have to pay to get on but one road and that's the bluegrass so you think. There are so many conveniences on this road that we can not count them. Everything you might desire can be found on these well traveled roads. Relaxing camp sites, places to party, places to shop, fast food restruarants, elegant restaurant, hotels, motels, rest areas, gas stations at nearly every other exit and phones along the way for ready assistance. Sometimes if you get lost there are people who are more willing to help along these well traveled roads than on the toll road.

On the toll road you may go for miles before you can find an exit or a place of rest. Sometimes it is better to make sure you have a tank full of gas because the filling stations are so far apart. That is the way it is on this christian journey. You must stop at your fueling station which is the word of God and the Holy Spirit will constantly replenish it when necessary if you have bathe yourself in his word. You must learn to discipline yourself not to get off on the by passes of life.

Rather when discouragement or weariness come upon you just keep going and keep the faith that as you journey along all that you need will be supplied. God will send you the right provisions you need to complete your journey. Sometimes you may fill that you will run out of fuel but at the right time the Holy spirit will replenish you. You may get tired but keep on going for there is a resting place ahead.

The toll road often is difficult to ask for directions if you feel that you are lost. Usually when you get on the toll road it is a fixed price to get to a designated place. Though the place you are going to seem far and no one seem to be traveling that road at times you still cannot stray too far off course because you have a fixed place to go. On our toll road the destination is heaven and eternal life the price fixed is paid by Jesus and the ultimate price was His life. The journey may be long and oftentimes tiring. There maybe many trials and obstacles along this road. Sometimes you may wonder if you will ever see a rest area or fueling station, but if you have disciplined yourself in prayer which is your vehicle, faith which is the mechanism that makes it turn and the studying of his word is the guiding force that will lead you by his Holy Spirit that abides in you.

"RUSH TO SORROW"

Genesis 42:38
And he said, My son shall not go down with you; for his
brother is dead, and he is left alone: if mischief befall him
by the way in the which Ye go, then will ye bring down my
gray hairs with sorrow to the grave.

Sorrow is a deep and lasting sadness or mental pain felt for misfortune, sin, the loss of someone dear to us.

In life often we make choices without consideration of the consequences. Sometimes if we just stop to think or pray before we rush into action we can prevent the sorrow that results from it. If Adam or Eve had considered that which the Lord had commanded then I don't believe Eve would've been tempted. If she had obeyed with reverence that which was told her upon creation then the fall of mankind would not have occurred and the sorrow that exist today would not be. When she hearken to the voice of satan and the deception of words were so strong and tempting she forgot what God had already given her and desired that which she could not obtain. Since that one willful act of disobedience man has continually rushed to sorrow.

Man has not looked at the deception of satan because they have not hearken unto the word of God. When Satan deceived Eve she in turn seduced her husband into being disobedient. Eve first act was not that of disobedience but one of coveting. She was coveting that which was not hers. Eve took a chance on what Satan said over the voice of God. Man can be given paradise and still desire more, desire of that which seems to be better or that which belongs to someone else. Much sorrow have entered into our lives because of covetousness.

Cain, had he made a more worthy sacrifice then he would not have been jealous of his brother Abel's sacrifice. Abel would not have been killed. That one act of deception and covetousness caused the whole of mankind to fall into the death of sin. Eve soon began to know and realize the zest of what she had done. Cain received a curse instead of a blessing because of this sin. A decision made in haste and through jealousy changed the direction of a whole nation of people.

If Abraham had not hearken unto the voice of his wife Sarah and trusted God to make good on His promises then the child of Hagar would not be an adversary with the child of promise. Sarah saw the sorrow that would be caused by this hasty decision before Ishmael was born. Yet the decision had been made the action had been done and a child was going to be born. The result Ishmael and Hagar were cast out resulting in a bitterness and resentment that would last forever.

We do not consider or ponder on that which we are about to do. We do not pray and seek God's divine guidance as David did before he went into battle. David always came out victorious when he sought the counsel of God. Saul offered a sacrifice without Samuel as a result he lost the throne to David. Acting in haste rushes us to sorrow. When we are confronted with a decision of temptation, we must seek God's divine intervention. When taking it upon ourselves to resolve or take action in a matter without consulting God in prayer can cause us much sorrow. Many times we only look at the pleasure and financial gain we sometime acquire never looking beyond the immediate results. However at times the action can result in pleasure for those directly involved usually the consequences affects a multitude of people and the sorrow last forever.

When a young woman knowingly seeks the affection of a married man desiring to break or tear apart a covenant that God has designed causes grief to the family and in the end grief to herself. When either partner breaks the covenant that God has designed causes much sorrow. David (the king) knew that Bathsheba was married and yet he broke the covenant of marriage between she and her husband. Resulting in the death of one of his trusted men. Thereby causing grief that would last forever in his family lineage.

As Christians we must learn to discipline ourselves and our children not to rush to sorrow. We rush to sorrow when we do not train our children up in the way they should go. When we stop following God's method of training but rather the intellect of man we are raising a society of individuals that will have no respect for home, community and church. We must prayerfully seek God in our daily walk, in the daily and hourly raising of our children. The scripture states: "In all thy ways acknowledge him, and he shall direct thy paths." Be not wise in thine own eyes : fear the Lord, and depart from evil." Proverb 3:6-7 If we read his word and prayerfully seek his guidance then the sorrows brought on by self will be very few. If we discipline our lives with the word of God and heed to the Holy Spirit that abides within then self inflicted sorrows will be few. If we take the time to teach our children the way the bible tells us to then our society would not be filled with the criminal environment we are in today. The lack of godly training in the home has caused parents to be slaughtered by their offspring. Because if we do not learn them of Jesus then they are open to the learning of the world which is ruled by satan for a time.

TREAD THE BEATEN PATH

Jeremiah 6:16
Thus saith the Lord, Stand ye in the ways, and see, and
ask for the old paths, where is the good way, and walk
therein, and ye shall find rest for your souls.

In the country we often find paths to take. Sometimes these paths are taken to keep us off the main road away from some of the dangers on the wide open road. Some paths are clear others are leaves and underbrush. The well treaded paths are usually the ones that are clear with few branches or stumps along the way.

Often as we walk this path you'll see where a snake has crossed or some less harmless animal. maybe the smell of a skunk lying in the underbrush. However no matter how well the path has been treaded we will still meet some of the obstacles that the original path maker confronted. Only now we can see more clearly what lies in our path. The path is easier for us because we have the path finder to follow.

Christians are on a path that has been well treaded. The path has been beaten clear by those who have treaded before. Enoch, a man who walked with God and was not, had learned how to talk and walk with God, and follow the hidden path of his heart. Noah believed and walked the hidden path of his heart. Abraham listened to the voice of God and walked out on faith. David a man after God's own heart, followed the unseen path that abided in his heart.

As we study our bibles and heed the words of God and listened with our ears open to the discipline of the Holy Spirit we can follow the beaten path of righteousness. A path that was hewn out in eternity by the footsteps of Jesus. If we seek the paths of old and walk therein, we shall find rest. As Abraham walked that path he grew in his faith, grew in courage, understanding, and wisdom. As David walked in that path be became very courageous in battle for the Lord. As a shepherd boy he was alone to communicate with God. There was a hidden strength in David that his father nor his brothers knew about. David was thought to be the lessor of the sons. However God knew the heart and courage of David. David had walked the path of a shepherd. He was the keeper of his earthly father's sheep. His brothers were the warrior and finer built men so Samuel and his father thought that one of them would be the anointed one. But God looked into the heart of David and chose him.

In our walk with Christ, we must first learn how to communicate with him. Our communication must be in the studying of his word, and prayer. Prayer is the key to walking the beaten and tried path of righteousness. There is no other way we can walk this path but in Jesus footsteps. If we try to walk Noah's footsteps we may become drunken along the way and lose sight of our goal. If we look at Abraham's footsteps we may act in haste and doubt that God is able to fulfill His promise through us because of age. If we look at David's footsteps we may look at our positions in life and become at ease and take that which belongs to another. But if we follow Jesus and realize that Noah, Abraham and David were following the footsteps of Jesus yet unseen but that it was promised them we can live a rich full life. These men of old made mistakes as we all do so therefore we cannot walk in their footsteps less we fall by the wayside.

We as christians must be careful not to follow the path of others to try to reach heaven. It is only through the blood of Jesus Christ are we able to reach the throne of Grace. On this path that we travel, we will bare a cross. We will be ridiculed, scorned, persecuted and abused. Sometimes our persecution will come through those we love and have chosen as our own intimate friend. We sometimes will be ridiculed by friends and forsaken by love ones. But as we walk this path we will see that Christ has taken the deadly wounding of these afflictions and healed them. We as christians have the abiding comforter of the Holy Spirit that can and will heal our wounding.

On this path we maybe raised upon a cross of trials and afflictions, thorns of worries and fears maybe placed around our head, nails of lack, want and distress maybe placed in our hands. Nails of discouragement and oppression maybe placed in our feet, piercings of rejection, denials, scorn, abuse and woundings of the spirit maybe stuck in our sides. But we know that Jesus has already suffered that for us. He has the healing salve of love that will bless us, strengthen us, and keep us, so we can suffer the cross and come through unscaled.

There is a resting time for us as we walk this path of righteousness. There is one who will help us bare the load that we carry. Jesus is the one on this path. Though unseen by the naked eye, we can feel him, strengthen, renew and direct us as we journey on. If one tells us that there is no lack or want of material things on this path they are deceivers. If one tells you that speaking out what we want and taking it or claiming it will give us our heart desires, they are deceivers. Christ spoke out love, forgiveness, grace and mercy for us to claim. In seeking His Will in our lives we must strive to be like Him. Only by walking the path that Jesus tread can we be like him. As we walk this path we will grow in his word. While growing we will learn that Christ lived a discipline life. He came for one purpose, that was to do His Father's will. As he prayed in the Garden of Gethsemane he cried out and spoke none the less let thine will be done. When the trials of life and discouragement, persecution and affliction come upon us and we've fervently prayed until the sweat runs down pleading with God to deliver us and spare us of the trials that come on us. We must also be discipline with the faith to say none the less let thy will be done. We can learn from the prophets of old by reading His Word. However learning to walk the beaten path that he cleared for us and daily walking close to him we learn of Him and through His Holy Spirit how to apply our daily experiences to make us more discipline in our walk with him.

WORKING IN HIS VINEYARD

Matthew 20:1-28

All things done well and effectively requires work. To till our soil we must work, to clean our house we must work. To pursue excellence in our chosen fields we must work. To be a good christian, parent, or teacher we must discipline ourselves and work. A vineyard requires much labor for the upkeep of it.

The disciples were followers of Christ. They learned from him. They saw him heal, raise the dead, feed the hungry, teach man and many other miracles that he performed. Christ visible work was done after he became an adult. He was at the age where parental rule was no longer effective, but the will of His Heavenly Father. The cause or purpose for which he had come was ready. But in the invisible from birth through mankind he was working in the vineyard preparing for the task set before him. He was an obedient child a caring and respectful child. These things were accounted to him showing that even as a child he was working in his vineyard.

In Proverbs 22: 6 "Train up a child in the way he should go and when he is old he will not depart from it." If a child is trained in an obedient way then even as a child he will show forth the fruits of labor in his vineyard. Christ attitude was of an obedient yet wise and godly child. Jesus built a bridge through out his mortal life showing forth his light. He laid a firm foundation.

"Let no man despise thy youth; but be thou an example of the believers, in word, in conversations, in charity, in spirit, in faith, in purity." I Timothy 4:12. We are admonished to be an example even in our youth, for we are to let no man despise our youth. Accepting Christ at an early age is an added advantage for it gives us a chance to learn and grow during our developing years. Even as a child while yet being disciplined by parents, while the rod of chastisement both morally and spiritually can open their ears; they can be working in the vineyard. Tender plants are planted in the vineyard and are nurtured and trained to be productive fruit bearing vines. The vines that are not fruitful or are weak or entwined with some weed is pruned or cut away so as to not hinder the growth of the fruitful ones.

God did not liken his laborers to the farmers nor the gardeners. The farmer has to cultivate and decide what will grow best in each field. The gardener has to be alert and fast acting as to not allow his garden to be over crowded with weeds. A vineyard once planted can last through generations if properly cared for. God liken our works as those that are done in his vineyard. In the vineyard once planted the grapes will grow as long as the vineyard have workers that are caring for the vineyard in the right way.

We as Christians are placed into the world through birth. We are placed in Christ vineyard through regeneration. Each laborer in this vineyard has a purpose. We are not there just to stand and watch others with criticism or gossiping. In this vineyard we must strive not to till the soil of others or become assassins of others character or work that they are striving to do. We cannot work effectively or help others by slothful and resentful attitudes. In the vineyard trees are not allowed to be planted around others as they are working for we cause the sun not to shine and the fruits of the vineyard can not be beneficial for they will grow to small or not at all due to the lack of sunshine. We must learn to dress properly so that we can work and not worry about the heat of the day. In the vineyard there is a season of rest before the harvest is ready for reaping. In our lives there is a season of rest before we embark upon another journey. During that time of rest we must prepare ourselves for the time of reaping. We must labor in prayer and in the word of God so that when it is time to reap the harvest our fruit will be ready for the plucking so we can have a productive increase.

Our heart is Christ vineyard. Our lives and the works that we do can only be as pure as the heart. The Holy Spirit is the tiller that tills the soil of our heart. As we work in the vineyard that Christ has placed us in he works within us to chicle out all things in our lives that will hinder us from being an effective worker. Sometimes without our ears being open to the proper discipline and we fail to read our bibles, or listen to the word of God, and our prayer life go unwatered we find ourselves getting weak or going astray. At times we fail to cry out Master careth thou not that we perish, we fail to work diligently in pursuit of excellence in our work. We become offenders and cause our fellow laborers harm. We daily lash out with our tongues words that causes wounding to the spirit and heart of sisters and brothers in Christ. While we are busy judging and planting groves around the heart of others we fail to look with in and clean our own house. When we are prayerful and study the word of God we become more careful of our actions toward others and we can feel the bonding of love that is required to live as true children of God. We labor to be perfect.

Matthew 5:48. "Be ye therefore perfect, even as your
Father which is in heaven is perfect"

For in our season of life, while we are yet able we must labor diligently in His vineyard so that the fruit of service and praise we give up to him will be as sweet wine in the harvest. We must strive not to offer up strange fires on the altar of our heart as we work in this vineyard. Because we cannot work effectively with a heart full of jealousy and envy neither can we work with the hardness of unforgiveness which causes us to look back frequently making our hearts become a pillar of salt. We must pull off the shoes of gossiping, and murmuring concerning the shepherd God has placed over us.

"The harvest truly is great, but the laborers are few: pray ye therefore the Lord of the harvest, that He would send forth laborers into his harvest." Luke 10:2 We cannot go out unprepared as Christ says that" He sends us forth as lambs among wolves" but we are not unprepared because his Holy Spirit abides in us. But many times we allow the spirit of jealousy and envy to intrude in our lives therefore another laborer falls by the wayside we cannot do soul winning. There are many souls that go lacking for the word of God because we as christians allow so many other things to take precedent over the true work God desires for us to do. The visible church should be our place of worship and prayer and not that of the place where we consider ourselves working for God in our positions in church. If we are a choir member then our daily work should be of singing God praises to the lost and ministering songs to those that are sick and diseased. If we are mothers of the church then we should be out visiting and praying for those that are lost those that have gone astray, those that are discouraged, because the fervent effective prayer of the righteous availeth much. If we are deacons then we should be helpers to the shepherd God has placed over us by visiting the sick, ministering to those who are in need. If we are missionaries as every christian is a missionary for Christ we must seek daily and prayerfully for a lost soul. If we are Ushers and responsible for greeting those that enters the visible church then daily we should be greeting young boys and girls with a smile that says come know the man that I serve learn of him and come to the house of worship. If we are just one of those who come just to hear the word of God and never hold a position in church we still are responsible for telling someone about that man called Jesus. James 5: 13-15." Is any among you afflicted ? Let him pray. Is any merry? Let him sing psalms. Is any sick among you? Let him call for the elders of the church: and let them pray over him, anointing him with oil in the name of the Lord: And the prayer of faith shall save the sick." We as christian must learn to be faithful so our prayers will not be hindered. James 5:19

"Brethren, if any of you do err from the truth, and one convert him: Let him know, that he which converteth the sinner from the error of his way shall save a soul from death, and shall hide a multitude of sins." Our work in His vineyard requires us to be prayerful and study his word. Only then can our ears be open for discipline.

SUMMARY

Everyday of our lives should be centered around the discipline that we can apply in our daily walk with Christ. As we strive daily to grow closer to him, praying and studying His Word are essential tools that we need for the discipline that our lives require. When we Bond in love with Christ we become workers in his vineyard. To work efficiently we must learn how to dress ourselves so that we can show forth Christ in our lives and not look down trodden. If we study the word of God and seek his guidance in our daily walk we can heed to the discipline that our spirit receives.

BVG